THE PSYCHOLOGY OF MONEY

UNDERSTANDING YOUR RELATIONSHIP WITH WEALTH AND HOW IT SHAPES YOUR FINANCIAL DECISIONS

Copyright@2024

Fedot Stanisler

TABLE OF CONTENT

- CHAPTER 1: THE CONCEPT OF MONEY 8
  - FIXED VERSUS GROWTH PERSPECTIVE IN FINANCIAL SUCCESS......................8
- CHAPTER 2: MONEY AND EMOTIONS 22
  - THE EMOTIONAL DRIVERS OF SPENDING AND SAVING 22
- CHAPTER 3: BEHAVIORAL BIAS AND INVESTMENT 33
  - DECISION MAKING................................33
- CHAPTER 4: THE PSYCHOLOGY OF INVESTING 43
  - RISK TOLERANCE IS THE ROOT OF HIS PSYCHE 43
- CHAPTER 5: MONEY, BEHAVIOR, AND TEMPERANCE....................................55
  - THE ROLE OF BEHAVIOR IN WEALTH CREATION...55
- CHAPTER 6: THE INFLUENCE OF SOCIAL FACTORS ON MONEY 68
  - KEEPING UP WITH THE JONESES............68
- CHAPTER 7: THE SCARCITY MINDSET AND FINANCIAL STRESS..........................74
  - THE PSYCHOLOGICAL EFFECTS OF DWELLING PAYCHECK TO PAYCHECK 74

INTRODUCTION

Money isn't just a number in a bank account or a bill in a wallet it's intimately connected to people's emotions, behaviors, and personalities. From our early experiences with it, money determines how we see ourselves and others, how we feel about success and security, and how we navigate the world. While financial literacy is important, the mindset of money—how we think and feel—is what really determines how we manage our money.

Most of us know what to do with money: save, invest and spend wisely. But when it comes to actual decision making, conscious feelings, attitudes, and beliefs often trump logic. Understanding these psychological factors is important for anyone looking to improve their financial situation, whether you're looking for wealth, financial freedom, or just peace of mind around money

Mastering the psychology of money is the key to financial success. By understanding how your mind works with money, you can make better choices, avoid common pitfalls, and ultimately be more satisfied and secure with your finances This book will be your guide to uncovering mind blocks of money and help you build a mindset of sustainable financial well-being.

Why money is psychological

Money is essentially a tool—a means of exchanging goods and services. However, its influence extends well beyond basic practices. Money carries emotional weight, symbolizing power, independence, security and even self-worth. For many people, how they handle money is not just about their financial skills, but about their mental state, upbringing, values, and past experiences. To understand why money is a psychological resource, we need to examine how deeply it is embedded in our personalities, emotions, and social interactions.

1. Wealth as sensory experience
- ❖ Money can trigger powerful emotions such as joy, fear, anxiety and guilt. For some, spending money provides instant gratification, a way to feel in control or relieve stress. For others, money is associated with fear—the fear of unworthiness or loss. These emotions often drive spending decisions, whether it's overspending, hoarding, or avoiding spending altogether. Understanding these emotional emotional triggers helps explain why even the most financially savvy can make poor financial decisions.

2. Baseline circumstances and money beliefs
- ❖ Our relationship with money often begins in childhood. The beliefs and practices we see from parents and

guardians form our first impressions of wealth, success, and security. These early lessons can determine whether we see money as a source of freedom or stress, and whether we embrace the idea of abundance or scarcity. For example, someone who was raised in an environment where money was always tight may develop a fear of financial distress, causing them to stick to savings or avoid risky investments when they may the more mature will be more willing to spend money or take financial risks.

3. Social Impact and Economic Comparison

❖ Money is also a social phenomenon. Our relationship with others is often determined by our view of them and their financial situation. Keeping up with the Joneses the cost of keeping up with or surpassing our peers is a familiar process motivated by a desire for social acceptance or recognition. This pressure can lead individuals to make financially unhealthy decisions, such as living beyond their means, incurring excessive debt, or risking more money to maintain their appearance

5. Wealth, self-worth, and identity

❖ For many people, money is their own value. Success is often determined by income, money, or material possessions, and financial failure can feel like a personal failure. This emotional attachment can cause stress, anxiety, and even shame about money. People avoid criticizing their finances or feel trapped by the demand for more money as a way to prove their worth to themselves and others.

6. Economic freedom and intellectual freedom
- ❖ The idea of financial freedom is not just about having enough money; it's about the psychological relief that comes with it. When one feels financially secure
- ❖ They generally feel a sense of control and peace of mind. Conversely, financial instability can lead to stress, anxiety, and feelings of being trapped, which can affect not only decision-making, but overall well-being.

CHAPTER 1: THE CONCEPT OF MONEY

FIXED VERSUS GROWTH PERSPECTIVE IN FINANCIAL SUCCESS

HOW MONEY BELIEFS SHAPE INVESTMENT DECISIONS

Our beliefs about money often instilled in us from childhood influence how we manage, spend, save, and invest. These beliefs act as a mental framework for interpreting financial situations, and can propel us towards financial success or lead to ongoing financial struggles How these beliefs shape our financial decisions common sense is crucial to change destructive systems and achieve better economic habits.

1. Scarcity versus abundance concept

One of the strongest beliefs influencing investment decisions is whether one operates with a scarcity or abundance mindset.

❖ Scarcity mindset: People with a scarcity mindset believe that resources are limited, and as a result they often make decisions out of fear out of fear. They stick to the money, avoid risk, and spend more when they don't even need to. This fear of not being enough can prevent them from pursuing opportunities such as investments or career advancement because they feel the potential loss is too risky For example, a person with a psychic rarely can avoid investing in stocks for fear of losing money, even though long-term growth can do so with their profits

- ❖ Abundance mentality: On the other hand, the abundance mentality is based on the belief that there are always enough resources and opportunities to go around. People with this type of confidence take calculated risks, invest in the future, and see setbacks as temporary. They tend to pursue wealth-building strategies such as entrepreneurship or real estate, believing that their efforts will pay off over time. This mindset can lead to better financial decisions such as saving and investing because one does not act from a place of fear.

2. Money as a source of security vs. security. source of freedom

For some, money represents security and comfort. This belief can lead to more conservative financial behaviors, such as excessive saving or avoiding debt altogether. While these can be wise decisions in many cases, taken to extremes, this mindset can lead to missing opportunities for growth or happiness

For others, money represents freedom a way to explore new opportunities, experiences, or lifestyles. These people are willing to spend a lot of money on travel, education, or starting a business because they see money as a means to a better life. However, if this belief leads to reckless spending without consideration for long-term security, the result can be financial disaster. Balancing security and autonomy is key to making sound investment decisions.

3. The role of preconditioning in money beliefs

- ❖ Our beliefs about money are often shaped by our upbringing and early experiences. If someone grew up in a household where money was always tight, they might believe that even with a higher income, that belief that financial hardship is inevitable can lead them to accumulate.

❖ In contrast, those who are older believe that money will always come quickly, which can lead to excessive spending or poor savings habits These people over-borrow or live beyond their means because they expect it that their economic status will always improve.

4. Beliefs about credit and risk

Beliefs about credit and financial risk play an important role in shaping investment decisions.

❖ It says it is bad: Some people are taught that all debt is bad and should be avoided at all costs. While this guarantee can help avoid unnecessary consumer debt, it can also prevent individuals from taking out "good debt" such as mortgages or student loans that can create long-term wealth, for example, by avoiding debt to start a business, even if it does, can be very profitable.

- ❖ Risk as fear: Many people believe that taking financial risks is risky and should be avoided. While caution is important, this belief can prevent individuals from engaging in wealth-creating activities such as investing in stocks, buying property, or starting a business Fear of risk often creates opportunities the potential for improvement is lost.
- ❖ Debt as a currency: Conversely, some people see debt as a tool for growth, especially if they believe in the power of using other people's money to create wealth This belief can lead to decision making such as investing in real estate or using debt for business purposes. Taking responsibility for these risks can lead to financial success. However, if a person

has excessive good faith about their debt, without knowing the risks involved, they can easily fall into bankruptcy by accumulating too much debt

5. Self-worth is money

- ❖ For many people, their belief in money is tied to their self-esteem and identity. Equating personal wealth with wealth, a person may make financial decisions based on the need for recognition or status. This can manifest itself in excessive spending on luxuries or sharing success and maintaining a lifestyle that they can't really afford. This belief can also lead to distress when money is tight, as they may personally feel inadequate during times of economic hardship.

On the other hand, those who do not tie their self-worth to money make decisions that prioritize long-term financial health over appearance.

POST-POVERTY PSYCHOLOGY AND PLURALISM

The concept of poverty and the concept of abundance go beyond mere economic status; They exhibit underlying concerns that significantly affect how individuals perceive and manage both resources, opportunities, and potential for improvement.

The Theory of Poverty

The concept of poverty, also known as the scarcity theory, is based on the belief that things whether wealth, opportunities, or success are scarce People with this concept see life as an empty game, where one must play fail and another wins. This belief constantly creates fear, insecurity and the need to protect what the few have, leading to short-term thinking and risk aversion

Main characteristics of poverty theory

1. Fear of loss and hoarding behavior

- ❖ Rare thinkers often fear that they will never have enough. This fear can lead to behaviors like hoarding money, possessions, and even time. Instead of using resources for development or investment, individuals focus on conserving them out of fear of future scarcity. This mindset may be holding them back from taking the financial risks necessary to build wealth, such as investing in education, starting a business, or entering a bank

2. Short-term thinking

- ❖ Scarcity of thought allows us to focus on immediate needs rather than long-term goals. For example, a person with a poverty mindset may be more inclined to spend money on entertainment or immediate needs rather than saving or investing for the future This can trap the person in a cycle of settling down paycheck to paycheck, where they can't escape their financial struggles

3. Limiting beliefs about rights

- ❖ A sense of poverty is also characterized by the belief that opportunities are scarce and difficult to obtain. This can manifest in feelings of jealousy or competition for the success of others as it reinforces the idea that there isn't enough to go around.

4. Effect of initial conditioning

- ❖ Many individuals develop a scarcity mindset based on their childhood experiences, especially if they grew up in an economically depressed environment. If a person was raised in a family where money was always scarce, they may be instilled with beliefs such as "money is hard" or "there is never enough". These deeply held beliefs can also carry over into adulthood, shaping their financial decisions even as their circumstances improve.

5. Stress and financial worries

❖   Living with a scarcity mindset leads to chronic stress and anxiety about money. Even with economic stability, people who favor poverty may feel insecure and worry about potential losses or future challenges. This can lead to overwork, excessive spending, or the inability to enjoy financial success because there is always the fear of losing what they have

Quantitative Thinking

❖ Abundance, in contrast, stems from the belief that there are always enough resources, opportunities, and success for everyone. People with this perspective see the world as full of possibilities, and they tend to tackle challenges with

optimism and creativity. This approach encourages long-term thinking, risk-taking, and empowerment over one's finances and personal future.
- ❖ Key characteristics of quantitative thinking:
1. Focus on opportunities and growth
- ❖ Individuals with a holistic mindset believe that opportunities are limitless. They see challenges as opportunities to grow and fail as a learning experience rather than a daunting tactic. This optimistic outlook motivates them to pursue new careers in business investment, or personal development, knowing that success is always within reach
2. Think long term and build wealth
- ❖ The concept of abundance helps in financial planning and long-term decision making. Rather than focusing

on immediate gratification, individuals with this mindset are more likely to invest in their future, save strategically, and plan for long-term goals that will retirement, education, job creation, etc. They understand that acquiring wealth requires patience and that small sacrifices today can yield big rewards tomorrow.

3. Kindness and cooperation

- ❖ The multifaceted mindset encourages the belief that success is not an empty game. Rather than competing with others or feeling threatened by success, people with this mindset tend to cooperate and give generosity. They believe that by helping others succeed, they contribute to an environment where everyone can succeed. This belief that everyone can succeed often leads to strong connections, relationships, and opportunities for personal economic growth.

4. Flexibility and risk taking

- ❖ People with an abundance mindset are more willing to take calculated risks because they believe they can recover from setbacks. They understand that failure is part of the journey to success, and instead of avoiding risks out of fear, they embrace them as learning opportunities

CHAPTER 2: MONEY AND EMOTIONS

THE EMOTIONAL DRIVERS OF SPENDING AND SAVING

HOW FEAR, GREED AND STRESS AFFECT ECONOMIC CHOICES

Financial decisions are not just rational; They are often affected by emotions such as fear, greed and anxiety. These cognitive biases can lead to both irrational behaviors and behaviors that affect long-term economic well-being.

1. Fear and its impact on investment decisions

Fear is a powerful emotion when it comes to financial decisions. It stems from anxiety about loss, instability, or uncertainty, and often leads individuals to make overly cautious or reactive choices.

The main ways in which fear influences investment choices are:

❖ Fear of losing money often prevents people from taking even calculated risks. While caution with money is wise, too much fear can lead to missed opportunities, such as avoiding investing in stocks, real estate, or business Those who let fear control their decisions want to invest into a low-interest-rate portfolio to undermine the growth potential of a wide variety of investments

❖ Fear selling in the market when the market is down:

❖ In an economic downturn or stock market downturn, panic can lead to panic selling. Many investors lose assets when the market goes down, motivated by the fear of further decline in prices. This behavior is known as loss aversion, and it often leads to losses being closed and losses that can be recovered as the markets recover.

Non-activity due to research paralysis:

❖ Panic can also lead to assessment paralysis, where individuals are so overwhelmed by potential risks and uncertainty about financial decisions that they do nothing at all Whether delaying investment, avoiding setting up a pension plan, employment not following through, fear of failure or making the wrong choice.

Excessive savings or hoarding:

❖ Fear of financial insecurity can lead to excessive accumulation or accumulation of wealth. While savings is a good financial habit, focusing too much on any investment can prevent a person from enjoying life or investing in experiences or opportunities that can enhance their well-being and improved future wealth.

2. Corruption and its role in economic decision making

❖ Greed, an excessive desire to make money can lead to unnecessary risk taking in order to maximize returns. Greed often overshadows judgment, leading people to prioritize short-term gain over long-term stability.

Follow along for a quick return:

❖ Greed pushes individuals to pursue high-return investments without fully understanding the risks involved. This behavior is often seen during stock market bubbles or with speculative investments or risky startups like cryptocurrencies. The promise of quick profits leads people to overlook sound investment principles like diversification, resulting in huge losses when markets inevitably take a right turn

Over leverage and debt accumulation:

❖ Greed can lead to excess capital—to borrow money to invest in high-risk projects in the hope of increasing profits. While this approach may work in a saturated market, it adds financial fragility. If investments don't perform as expected, debt can spiral out of control, resulting in significant financial losses or even bankruptcy.

Holding onto investments for too long:

❖ "Fear of missing out" (FOMO) and greed often keep individuals investing for too long, hoping for high returns, even when the market is clearly up This behavior can lead to missed opportunities taking huge gains and losses when the market does well or crashes It can.

Unethical Financial Practices:
- ❖ In extreme cases, corruption can lead individuals to engage in unethical or illegal financial practices, such as fraud or insider trading, in pursuit of wealth Although these practices can generate short-term benefits though with significant legal and moral ramifications.

3. Stress and financial decisions
- ❖ Financial stress is especially common during times of economic hardship, job loss, or personal financial crisis. Chronic stress can impair judgment, leading to rash or passive decision making.

Aggressive spending:
- ❖ Stress often triggers rapid spending to cope with anxiety or problems. Emotional spending on unnecessary things—such as shopping, eating out, or buying luxury goods—can provide temporary relief from stress but often

exacerbates financial problems long-term, especially when people are financially constrained and seek short-term satisfaction

Dealing with emotional costs and guilt related to money

Emotional costs and guilt related to money are common challenges that can get in the way of financial stability and well-being. Emotional costs often come from stress, boredom, or the desire for immediate gratification, while guilt comes from making financial decisions that are not aligned with long-term goals.

1. Understanding the emotional cost

Emotional spending is the act of buying based on emotion rather than need. People often use shopping as a way to cope with negative emotions or celebrate positive emotions, without considering the financial consequences.

Common triggers for emotional spending:

- ❖ Stress or anxiety: Shopping can provide temporary relief from stress, anxiety, and other overwhelming emotions. However, this relief is short-lived, and the financial burden of overspending can cause stress in the long run.
- ❖ Boredom: Many people turn to shopping as a form of entertainment when they are bored, using purchases to fill an emotional or mental void.
- ❖ Low self-esteem: Emotional costs can be linked to self-esteem issues. Some people buy luxuries or frills to increase their self-worth or to gain the approval of others.
- ❖ Celebrate and reward: Shopping can also be a way to celebrate its own accomplishments or reward hard work, but doing it too soon can lead to financial regrets

2. Steps to manage emotional costs

❖ Breaking the cycle of emotional spending requires a combination of self-awareness, discipline, and creating a supportive financial environment.

Acknowledge the emotional trigger:

❖ The first step in dealing with emotional spending is to identify the emotional triggers that precipitate purchases. Think about the emotions that arise before the purchase—are you stressed, nervous, bored, or trying to get over your feelings? Once you recognize these feelings, you can begin to address them without resorting to spending money.

Make a budget and stick to it:

❖ Establishing a healthy budget helps with boundaries and accountability. Set a specific amount for non-essentials like eating out or shopping, and stick to that limit. Knowing how much you can spend on things you want reduces the likelihood of buying things you want.

Use the "Cooling Off" period:

❖ Apply a cooling rule to purchases. For example, wait 24 to 48 hours before making any purchases. This delay gives you time to investigate whether you really need or want the item, reducing the likelihood of emotional spending or a quick bill.

Use Mental Spending:

❖ Mindful spending allows you to be more aware of your spending habits and make deliberate choices based on your financial goals. Before making a purchase, ask yourself if the item matches your priorities or if it is just a temporary emotional fix. Using discretion when shopping helps reduce impulsive decisions.

Find out the best ways to cope:

❖ Instead of using shopping as a coping mechanism, find other ways to deal with emotions. Exercising, journalism, talking to a friend, or using relaxation techniques can provide relief from stress or anxiety without affecting your finances.

The waste table:

❖ Monitor your spending to better understand where your money is going. By reviewing your expenses on a regular basis, you become more aware of your emotional costs and can adjust accordingly. Apps or financial tools that categorize expenses can help track.

CHAPTER 3: BEHAVIORAL BIAS AND INVESTMENT

DECISION MAKING

STRATEGIES FOR IDENTIFYING AND COMBATING ECONOMIC BIAS

Economic biases are cognitive shortcuts or systematic deviations from norms or logic in judgment that can affect decision-making. This bias can lead to poor financial choices, affecting savings, investment and spending.

1. Awareness and instruction

Understand common financial biases:

- ❖ Anchoring bias: over-reliance on prior information (e.g., initial values) when making a decision.
- ❖ Loss aversion: the tendency to prioritize avoidance of loss over equivalent gain; The pain of loss is more powerful psychologically than the pleasure of gain.

- ❖ Overconfidence bias: overestimating one's knowledge or ability to predict outcomes, potentially leading to risky investments.
- ❖ Freshness Bias: Disproportionate weight is given to recent information or experiences by ignoring historical events or trends.

Teach yourself:

- ❖ Learn about economic biases and their impact on decision making. Recognizing when biases are influencing your choices is a powerful tool.

2. Use structured decision-making processes

Use search criteria:

- ❖ Develop a checklist for investment decisions including objective criteria. This can help you consider all relevant factors and minimize the emotional impact.

Set clear goals:

Set specific, measurable financial goals. When making a decision, refer back to these goals and see if your options align with your long-term goals.

Project Decision Forms:

Create a decision journal to record key financial decisions. Write down the reasoning behind your choice, how you feel at the time, and the consequences. A review of this journal can help identify mechanisms of bias over time.

3. Explore ideas

Discuss with others:

- ❖ Get input from friends, family members, or trusted financial advisors when making important financial decisions. Perspectives can reveal potential biases and expand your understanding.

Join financial groups or forums:

❖ Participate in investment groups or seminars to gain insight into experiences and perspectives. This can challenge your assumptions and give you new options.

4. Objective emphasis

Rely on data analysis:

Base your investment decisions on data, trends, and analytics tools instead of gut feeling.

Set boundaries on emotional decisions:

Make rules for yourself, such as waiting time before making important purchases or investing. This gives them time to think the decision through rationally.

5. Observation and reflection

Review investment decisions regularly:

Review your financial decisions and consequences from time to time. Consider whether bias influenced your choice and how it can be counteracted in the future.

Practicing mindfulness:

Engage in mindfulness practices to become more aware of money-related thoughts and feelings. Attention can help identify emotional triggers and biases in real time.

6. Have a growth mindset

Accept mistakes as learning opportunities:

Instead of feeling guilty about financial mistakes, look at them as learning experiences. This cognitive shift can reduce the effects of biases such as loss aversion and overconfidence.

Stay open to customization:

Be willing to adjust your financial plans based on new information or changing circumstances. These changes can help reduce the biases associated with aggressiveness or overconfidence.

Real Life examples of biased investment decisions

Economic biases can have a profound effect on our decision-making processes, often leading to outcomes that may be contrary to our best interests.

1. Anchor bias

Example: home buying decisions

When buying a home, potential buyers can base their price expectations on a listing or a first home. If they see a home listed at $300,000, they may focus on that figure when considering other properties, leading to meaningless comparisons and decisions. For example, they may overlook the same $280,000 home, which they think is "too low" relative to their anchor. This bias can result in the property being overpaid or losing quality.

2. Hating injuries

Example: stock market behavior

Investors generally exhibit loss aversion and fear the pain of losing money more than the pleasure of making money. During a market downturn, an investor may hold a loss-making stock, hoping not to suffer a loss even when evidence suggests it may not recover For example, one may stick to a stock market one that has dropped $50 towards $20, and has believed that the sell off will cement a loss, of investing in more promising stocks Opportunities disappear

3. Overconfidence is negative

Examples: start-ups and projects

Entrepreneurs often exhibit overconfidence in their business ideas. For example, a developer may believe that their product will succeed based on their interests or past experience, thus underestimating competition and market challenges marketing or production without adequate market research, resulting in economic failure

4. Novelty bias

Example: investment decisions

An investor may be affected by recent market trends, which may cause recent biases. If a particular sector, such as technology, has seen rapid growth, an investor may ignore historical performance and valuations and pour money into technology stocks. For example, in a technological boom, an investor might buy a bullish stock based solely on recent performance, neglecting to consider long-term fundamentals, a it could cost him a big loss as the market corrects

5. Animal Practice

Example: Cryptocurrency investment

In a cryptocurrency boom, individuals tend to follow the crowd, due to their desire not to miss out on potential profits. For example, in late 2017, many investors rushed to buy bitcoin and other cryptocurrencies as prices rose, ignoring underlying risks and volatility This conservative behavior led to a sharp rise in prices, followed by an active correction that saw many investors incur substantial losses.

6. The price of the dip is wrong

Example: Continuing a failed task

The sunk cost fallacy occurs when individuals continue to invest time, money, or resources in a failed venture because they have already invested in it, rather than evaluating future possibilities It turns out that this bias can result in additional losses.

7. Mental Accounts

Example: budgets and expenditures

Mental accounting involves allocating money into buckets, which can lead to irrational financial decisions. For example, a person can view their tax refund as "fun money" without viewing it as part of their overall financial picture. They may borrow or spend more easily for pleasure rather than saving for emergencies, resulting in poor economic performance.

8. Emphasis bias

Example: investment strategies

Investors often exhibit a confirmation bias by ignoring contradictory information and looking for information that supports their existing beliefs about investing e.g., a convincing investor as a particular company one can read and analyze only positive news and reject bad news.

CHAPTER 4: THE PSYCHOLOGY OF INVESTING

RISK TOLERANCE IS THE ROOT OF HIS PSYCHE

WHY PEOPLE ARE AFRAID TO INVEST AND HOW TO DEAL WITH IT

Investing can be a powerful way to grow wealth over the long term, but many individuals are very afraid of entering the financial sector. This fear is often the result of a combination of emotional, **psychological, and practical factors.** Understanding these fears and implementing strategies to overcome them can empower individuals to make informed financial decisions.

1. Why they are afraid to invest

1.1 Lack of knowledge and understanding

- Many people are afraid to invest because they lack the necessary knowledge or understanding of financial markets. This uncertainty can lead to feelings of inadequacy and hesitation.

1.2 Fear of loss
- Fear of losing money is one of the most important deterrents to investing. Market fluctuations can be unpredictable, and many individuals worry about the possibility of significant losses.

1.3 Market Changes
- Natural fluctuations in the stock market can create disturbing results. Large changes in prices can make individuals cautious, leading them to believe that investing is more like gambling than rational financial planning.

1.4 Past experiences
- Individuals who have lost money in the past, whether through poor investments

or market downturns, may have a permanent fear of investing in. These experiences can create a psychological barrier seeds that are difficult to control.

1.5 Influence of media and society

- ❖ Media images of market crashes or stories of individuals losing their life savings can fuel fear. In addition, friends and family may express skepticism or caution about investing, further reinforcing negative feelings.

1.6 Equality and Evaluation Paralysis

- ❖ The desire to make the "perfect" investment can lead to analytical paralysis, where one overestimates and hesitates in making decisions. This can be due to the fear of making a mistake or not getting the best results.

2. Ways to overcome fear of investing

2.1 Introduce yourself

- ❖ Knowledge gives power. Taking the time to learn about investments, market concepts, and risk management can boost your confidence. Resources include books, online courses, podcasts, and financial reporting organizations.

2.2 Start short

- ❖ Start with the smallest amount you can afford. This gives you experience without taking too much risk. As you get more comfortable with the investment, you can gradually increase the investment.

2.3 Diversify your investments

- ❖ Diversification can help reduce risk by spreading investments across asset classes. A diversified portfolio can reduce the impact of market fluctuations on your overall financial situation, giving you greater peace of mind.

2.4 Set clear objectives

❖ Set specific, realistic financial goals that inform your spending decisions. Knowing why you're investing—like retirement, a home, or education—can give you motivation and clarity of purpose, making your investments feel more manageable

2.5 Creation of emergency funds

❖ Having a solid emergency fund can reduce some of the fear associated with investing. Knowing you have financial security in place can give you the confidence to invest without having to worry about your immediate financial needs.

2.6 Seek professional guidance

❖ Consider working with a financial advisor or planner. A qualified professional will be able to give you practical guidance, help you develop a sound financial plan, and answer your questions and address your concerns.

2.7 Focus on long-term results

- ❖ Shift your focus from short-term volatility to long-term economic performance. Historically, markets have shown positive momentum over long periods of time, and holding long-term can help reduce concerns about day-to-day market fluctuations

2.8 Use cognitive and emotional intelligence

- ❖ Recognize and acknowledge your fears about investing. Mindfulness can help eliminate negative emotions, enabling more rational decision making. Techniques such as journaling or meditation can help manage these feelings.

2.9 Join various investment teams

❖ Getting involved in communities, forums, or groups that focus on finances can provide support and encouragement. Sharing experiences and learning from others can help demystify the financial system and build trust.

A LONG-TERM PERSPECTIVE THAT WILL MAKE A GOOD INVESTMENT

Being a long-term thinker is critical to investing. This approach focuses on growth and value over time rather than reacting to short-term market fluctuations. Key principles and strategies for developing a long-term financial outlook include:

1. Embrace collective power

Complex reason:

Compounding refers to the process by which the return on an investment earns its own return over time. If you continue to invest for a long time, this great growth can significantly increase your income.

Before they begin:

The earlier you start investing, the longer it takes for your money to grow. Even small contributions can add up significantly over time, demonstrating the importance of starting right away.

2. Set clear, long-term goals

Define your goals:

Set specific financial goals, such as retirement, buying a home, or funding education. Having a clear goal guides your financial decisions and helps keep you focused and confident.

Time frame:

Consider investing time. Longer periods may allow for more aggressive investment strategies, while shorter periods may require a more aggressive approach to risk mitigation.

3. Create a diversified portfolio

Risk management:

❖ Diversification involves spreading investments across different asset classes (stocks, bonds, real estate, etc.) to reduce risk. A well-diversified portfolio can help prevent market volatility.

Asset distribution:

❖ Determine the right asset allocation based on your risk tolerance, investment objectives and time horizon. Regularly review and adjust your portfolio to stay aligned with long-term goals.

4. Stay informed and educated

Continuing Education:

Stay informed on markets, economic indicators and investment strategies. Knowledge enables you to make informed decisions and adapt to changing circumstances without fear.

Avoid emotional investing:

❖ Educate yourself about the common cognitive biases and emotional pitfalls of investing. Being informed helps reduce panic and irrational decision making during market downturns.

5. Maintain discipline and consistency

Regular Contributions:

❖ Use a systematic investment strategy such as dollar cost averaging, where you typically invest a certain amount, regardless of market conditions. This approach reduces the impact of market fluctuations and encourages discipline.

Stick to your plan:

❖ Create a budget based on your goals and risk tolerance. Avoid making rash changes in response to short-term market developments. Reassess only as necessary and stick to your plan.

6. Be patient and flexible

Long-term outlook:

Understand that investing is a marathon, not a sprint. Market volatility is normal, and focusing on long-term growth can help you ride out the booms and busts.

Resilience to market fluctuations:

Accept that market volatility is part of investing. Having resilience allows you to withstand lower volatility without making wild sells, and allows you to take advantage of market rebounds.

7. Review and adjust periodically

Regular portfolio reviews:

Review your investment periodically and see how it's performing against your goals. Make necessary adjustments based on changes in life circumstances, investment goals, or market conditions.

Rebalance if necessary:
- ❖ Rebalancing involves adjusting your portfolio to maintain your desired asset base. This exercise ensures that you are not too exposed to any one asset class, which helps you manage risk.

8. Focus on price, not time

Philosophy of long-term investing:

Focus on investing in quality assets with strong fundamentals rather than trying to time the market. Good investments tend to weather economic storms and appreciate over time.

Value Rating:

Consider taking a value-based approach by focusing on undervalued assets that have long-term growth potential. This approach often provides better long-term returns than trying to follow short-term trends.

9. Surround yourself with a supportive network

Get expert guidance:
- ❖ Consider working with financial advisors or joining investment groups. Their expertise can give you valuable insight and hold you accountable to a long-term strategy.

CHAPTER 5: MONEY, BEHAVIOR, AND TEMPERANCE

THE ROLE OF BEHAVIOR IN WEALTH CREATION

HOW TO DEVELOP HEALTHY MONEY HABITS AND HOW TO BREAK BAD ONES

Forming good financial habits and breaking bad ones are essential to achieving financial stability and growth.

1. Set clear financial goals

- ❖ Define your goals: Start by identifying short, medium, and long-term financial goals. Whether it's saving for a vacation, buying a home, or retirement, having clear goals provides motivation and direction.

- ❖ Make them SMART: Make sure your goals are specific, measurable, attainable, relevant, and timely. This clarity will help you track your progress and stay focused.

2. Make a budget

❖ Monitor your income and expenses: List all sources of income and break down your expenses to understand where your money is going. Use budgeting tools or apps to track quickly.

❖ Set spending limits: Assign a specific amount to each category and stick to those limits. This can help curb impulse spending and encourage mindful purchases.

3. Automate savings and payments

❖ Pay yourself ahead: Set up an automatic checking account as soon as you have money. Treat savings like a fixed cost to ensure priority.

❖ Automate bills: Schedule automatic payments to ensure timely payments and avoid being late. This reduces stress and helps maintain a good credit score.

4. Create an emergency fund

- ❖ Start small: Aim to save on living expenses for at least three to six months. Start with a small goal like saving $500, then gradually increase it.
- ❖ Use a separate account: Keep emergency funds in a separate, easily accessible account to prevent them from being used for non-emergencies.

5. Review and adjust regularly

- ❖ Regular checkins: Review your budget and financial goals regularly (monthly or quarterly) to monitor progress and make adjustments as needed.
- ❖ Celebrate milestones: Acknowledge and celebrate accomplishments along the way, no matter how small. This helps keep them motivated.

6. Have a budget in mind
- ❖ 24-hour rule: Use a waiting period before making unnecessary purchases. This helps you narrow down the list of purchases you want to make and gives you time to evaluate whether the purchase matches your goals.
- ❖ Distinguish between what you want and what you need: Identify what you really need and what you want. First, focus on satisfying needs and see if a desire is worth the cost.

7. Educate yourself about finances
- ❖ Read books and articles: Spend time learning about personal finance through books, blogs, podcasts, and online courses. Knowledge enables you to make informed decisions.
- ❖ Attend workshops or seminars: Attend financial literacy seminars to gain

practical knowledge and strategies for managing money effectively.

8. Identify and challenge negative beliefs about money

- ❖ Consider your money attitude: Identify any negative beliefs or attitudes you have about money (e.g., "I'll never be good with money"). Challenge these assumptions and replace them with positive affirmations.
- ❖ Practice gratitude: Acknowledge and appreciate what you have on a regular basis. This can shift your focus from scarcity to abundance and foster a healthy relationship with money.

9. Seek professional help if necessary

- ❖ Financial Advisors: Consider working with a financial advisor to get the right guidance and tailored strategies for your situation.

❖ Therapists or Coaches: If bad money habits are deeply rooted in emotional issues, seeking help from a therapist or financial coach can provide valuable insight and support.

10. Surround yourself with positive influences

❖ Join a supportive community: Connect with friends, family, or online groups focused on financial wellness. Sharing experiences and advice can motivate you to stick to good habits.

❖ Limit Bad Influences: Limit exposure to people or the media that promote improper financial practices or behavior.

Long-term satisfaction and economic value

Delayed gratification refers to the ability to resist the temptation to receive an immediate reward and wait for a later reward. This concept is often associated with better decision-making and overall success in various areas of life, especially in personal finance.

1. Understanding Delayed Gratification

Definition: Delayed gratification entails prioritizing long term advantages over instant pleasures. It calls for self control and the capacity to delay short term rewards for extra considerable profits inside the destiny.

- ❖ Psychological Basis: Research, along with the well-known Stanford marshmallow experiment, demonstrates that folks who can postpone gratification often experience more fulfillment and well being. They generally tend to make better life choices, inclusive of financial selections.

2. Financial Benefits of Delayed Gratification

2.1 Increased Savings and Wealth Accumulation

- ❖ Long Term Savings: By postponing instant spending, individuals can store extra cash. For instance, selecting to shop for a bigger purchase in place of shopping for smaller gadgets unexpectedly lets in for collecting wealth through the years.
- ❖ Compound Interest: The in advance and more continually you keep, the more you gain from compound interest. For example, investing a small amount regularly can grow notably over decades, leading to tremendous wealth via retirement.

2.2 Reduced Debt Levels

❖ Avoiding Impulsive Purchases: Delaying gratification helps people withstand impulse shopping for and useless costs. This can cause lower credit card debt and less reliance on loans, contributing to average monetary health.

❖ Smart Spending Decisions: By thinking about purchases cautiously and anticipating the proper second, individuals could make higher picks, ensuring they only spend money whilst it aligns with their financial desires.

2.3 Enhanced Financial Discipline

❖ Building Self Control: Practicing not on time gratification cultivates field, making it less complicated to stick to budgets and financial savings plans. This discipline interprets into healthier financial behavior through the years.

- ❖ Long Term Planning: Individuals who embody behind schedule gratification have a tendency to assume long term, main to higher economic planning. This consists of setting and achieving desires like home possession, retirement financial savings, or beginning a commercial enterprise.

2.4 Improved Investment Decisions

- ❖ Strategic Investing: Investors who practice delayed gratification are much less possibly to react swiftly to market fluctuations. They recognize that short term volatility is part of investing and awareness on long term growth capacity.
- ❖ Risk Management: With a long term mindset, individuals can take calculated dangers, leading to probably higher returns through the years as opposed to chasing short profits or panicking for the duration of marketplace downturns.

2.5 Greater Financial Security

❖ Emergency Funds: Delayed gratification encourages saving for emergencies in place of spending disposable earnings right away. Building an emergency fund presents a economic cushion at some stage in sudden conditions.

❖ Retirement Preparedness: Individuals who prioritize behind schedule gratification regularly make contributions more to retirement money owed, ensuring they've ok financial savings for his or her later years, main to monetary independence.

3. Strategies to Cultivate Delayed Gratification

3.1 Set Clear Financial Goals

❖ Define Priorities: Establish particular short term and long term financial dreams. Knowing what you're operating in the direction of assist you to withstand the temptation of instantaneous rewards.

3.2 Create a Budget

- ❖ Track Spending: Maintain a finances to reveal where your money goes. This consciousness permit you to identify areas in which you may postpone gratification to allocate budget toward your desires.

3.3 Practice Mindfulness

- ❖ Pause Before Spending: Implement a rule to attend 24 hours before making nonessential purchases. This practice lets in you to mirror on whether the purchase is essential and aligns together with your dreams.

3.4 Reward Yourself

- ❖ Incentive Delayed Gratification: Set up a system of small rewards for your self when you acquire a financial savings milestone or persist with your budget.

This can assist make stronger fine behaviors at the same time as retaining consciousness on long term dreams.

3.5 Surround Yourself with Positive Influences

- ❖ Supportive Environment: Engage with like minded folks that prioritize saving and investing. Their high quality behaviors can inspire and inspire you to practice behind schedule gratification.

CHAPTER 6: THE INFLUENCE OF SOCIAL FACTORS ON MONEY

KEEPING UP WITH THE JONESES

FINANCIAL PEER PRESSURE AND HOW TO RESIST IT

Financial peer stress refers back to the have an impact on that buddies, circle of relatives, or social organizations have on an character's economic behaviors and selections. This stress can lead to spending beyond one's approach, making impulsive purchases, or carrying out unhealthy financial practices. Understanding a way to face up to economic peer strain is crucial for maintaining economic stability and attaining personal financial desires.

1. Recognize Financial Peer Pressure

 Identify Sources: Be aware of who impacts your financial decisions. This should consist of friends who regularly dine out, own family members who have exclusive spending behavior, or social media influencers promoting lavish life.

- ❖ Understand the Impact: Acknowledge how peer stress impacts your spending habits. Are you buying things you don't want just to hold up with others? Recognizing these patterns is the first step to resisting them.

2. Set Clear Financial Goals

- ❖ Define Your Priorities: Establish specific short term and long term financial desires that replicate your values and aspirations. Knowing what you want to achieve can help you stay focused and much less swayed through outside influences.
- ❖ Create a Budget: Develop a budget that aligns with your dreams. A clear economic plan can offer a framework for

making knowledgeable spending decisions, making it less difficult to withstand peer stress.

3. Cultivate a Strong Money Mindset

- ❖ Focus on Value: Shift your mind-set from evaluating your self to others to comparing what genuinely brings you value and happiness. Prioritize reviews and purchases that align along with your desires in preference to those that fulfill social expectations.
- ❖ Practice Gratitude: Regularly reflect on what you're thankful for to your financial situation. This can help you admire what you've got and decrease the desire to comply to others' spending habits.

4. Communicate Your Financial Values

- ❖ Be Honest: Share your economic goals and values together with your friends and family. Being obvious about your priorities can help them apprehend your selections and reduce stress to spend.

Set Boundaries: If pals or family contributors inspire spending that conflicts along with your values, set up clear boundaries. Politely decline invites or recommend alternative sports that align along with your monetary goals.

5. Surround Yourself with Supportive Influences

- ❖ Choose Like Minded Friends: Seek relationships with those who proportion comparable financial values and goals. Having a supportive social circle can reinforce high quality monetary behaviors and provide motivation to stick on your dreams.
- ❖ Join Financial Groups: Consider joining businesses or communities focused on economic literacy or frugality. Engaging with those who prioritize saving and

budgeting can inspire you to withstand peer pressure.

6. Limit Social Media Exposure

- ❖ Curate Your Feed: Follow debts that promote monetary literacy, saving guidelines, and healthful spending behavior. Avoid influencers or content material that promotes excessive spending or materialism.
- ❖ Take Breaks: Consider taking breaks from social media if you locate yourself feeling pressured to hold up with others' life. Limiting publicity can assist reduce temptation and preserve consciousness for your own monetary dreams.

7. Practice Mindfulness in Spending

- ❖ Pause Before Purchases: Implement a rule to wait 24 hours earlier than making nonessential purchases. This pause can help you examine whether the object aligns with your desires or if it's an impulse pushed via peer strain.

❖ Reflect on Purchases: After making a buy, reflect on whether or not it changed into a considerate selection or a response to external pressures. This practice let you identify styles and regulate your behaviors for that reason.

8. Celebrate Small Wins

❖ Acknowledge Progress: Celebrate your monetary achievements, regardless of how small. Recognizing your progress reinforces fantastic behaviors and strengthens your commitment on your financial dreams.

❖ Share Your Successes: Share your monetary successes with supportive friends or family. This can help inspire them and create an environment in which prioritizing monetary health is celebrated in preference to forced.

CHAPTER 7: THE SCARCITY MINDSET AND FINANCIAL STRESS

THE PSYCHOLOGICAL EFFECTS OF DWELLING PAYCHECK TO PAYCHECK

HOW SCARCITY INFLUENCES DECISION MAKING

Scarcity, described because the confined availability of sources relative to the demand for the ones assets, extensively impacts decision making techniques. The concept of scarcity now not simplest applies to fabric assets however also extends to time, attention, and even cognitive bandwidth.

1. Focus on Short Term Gains
- ❖ Immediate Gratification: Scarcity frequently leads individuals to prioritize on the spot rewards over long term

benefits. When sources are perceived as limited, there's a bent to make decisions that offer quick pride in place of considering future outcomes.

❖ Impulsive Decisions: The strain of shortage can bring about impulsive selections, as individuals may additionally act quickly to secure what they understand as limited possibilities, every so often neglecting careful attention of capacity downsides.

2. Risky Behavior

❖ Increased Risk Taking: Scarcity can pressure human beings to take more risks in an attempt to acquire scarce resources. For example, people facing financial constraints may gamble or put money into high risk ventures to enhance their situation quickly.

- ❖ Overvaluing Limited Opportunities: When sources are scarce, individuals might overvalue them, main to decisions primarily based on urgency rather than rational assessment. This can bring about negative investment alternatives or purchases driven via fear of missing out (FOMO).

3. Reduced Cognitive Capacity

- ❖ Cognitive Overload: Scarcity can create a feel of cognitive load, making it difficult for people to method records correctly. When that specialize in on the spot scarcity, humans may forget important information and fail to don't forget all options.
- ❖ Tunnel Vision: Scarcity regularly narrows awareness, leading individuals to concentrate entirely at the scarce resource at the same time as ignoring different essential elements. This tunnel

imaginative and prescient can impede sound decision making and cause unbalanced selections.

4. Emotional Responses

- ❖ Stress and Anxiety: Scarcity can evoke feelings of pressure, anxiety, and desperation. These emotions can cloud judgment and lead to hasty or poorly thought out decisions, similarly exacerbating the shortage mind-set.
- ❖ Fear of Loss: The worry of dropping out on restrained resources can power human beings to make decisions based totally on worry instead of rationality. This may additionally result in hoarding behavior, excessive saving, or unplanned purchases.

5. Altered Value Perception

- ❖ Perceived Value Increase: When assets are scarce, their perceived fee tends to increase. This can lead people to pay extra for gadgets or offerings than they would in a context of abundance, as scarcity triggers a sense of urgency.

❖ Willingness to Compromise: In situations of scarcity, individuals may be more willing to compromise their standards or values to secure confined sources, leading to selections they won't make underneath distinctive instances.

6. Social Influences

❖ Social Comparison: Scarcity can make bigger social comparisons, wherein individuals gauge their selections based totally on others' get entry to to assets. This may additionally lead to feelings of inadequacy or pressure to comply to perceived social standards.

❖ Group Dynamics: In corporations facing shortage, decision making can become greater encouraged via social dynamics. Peer pressure and collective tension can exacerbate rushed selections or inspire riskier behaviors.

7. Long Term Consequences

- ❖ Neglecting Future Needs: Scarcity driven decision making regularly overlooks future effects. Individuals might also burn up resources inside the quick time period, ensuing in negative outcomes consisting of financial instability or aid depletion in the long run.
- ❖ Cycle of Scarcity: Poor selections made below shortage can perpetuate a cycle of shortage. For example, impulsive spending can result in financial stress, inflicting people to feel greater scarcity and make in addition bad choices.

BREAKING FREE FROM THE CYCLE OF FINANCIAL STRESS

Financial strain can create a relentless cycle of hysteria and pressure that influences not simplest your economic well being but also your typical fitness and relationships. Breaking free from this cycle requires a proactive approach to coping with your price range and addressing the underlying problems that make a contribution to stress.

1. Identify the Sources of Financial Stress

Assess Your Situation: Take a complete study your economic situation, together with earnings, charges, money owed, and savings.

- ❖ Recognize Triggers: Identify particular factors that cause monetary strain, such as sudden charges, activity insecurity, or dwelling beyond your means. Recognizing these triggers let you expand focused techniques to deal with them.

2. Create a Budget

Track Your Income and Expenses: Document all assets of profits and categorize your fees to gain a clear image of your financial go with the flow. This cognizance will assist you perceive regions in which you can reduce back or allocate extra effectively.

❖ Set Realistic Limits: Establish a budget that aligns together with your financial goals and reflects your real spending conduct. Ensure your finances lets in for critical charges at the same time as prioritizing savings and debt compensation.

3. Build an Emergency Fund

❖ Start Small: Aim to store a small, manageable quantity each month to construct an emergency fund. Start with a purpose of $500 and steadily paintings up to a few to 6 months' well worth of residing costs.

- ❖ Use a Separate Account: Keep your emergency fund in a separate, without problems reachable account. This will help you avoid the temptation to dip into it for non emergencies and provide a protection net during surprising situations.

4. Address Debt Wisely

- ❖ Prioritize Debt Repayment: Create a plan for tackling debt, focusing on high interest debts first (debt avalanche technique) or starting with smaller debts for brief wins (debt snowball technique). Choose a approach that feels doable for you.
- ❖ Negotiate with Creditors: Don't hesitate to attain out to lenders for ability relief options, such as lower interest charges or

prolonged price plans. Many lenders are inclined to paintings with you if you speak proactively.

5. Develop a Mindset of Abundance

- ❖ Shift Your Perspective: Focus on what you have in preference to what you lack. Practicing gratitude can help shift your attitude from scarcity to abundance, lowering anxiety round monetary assets.
- ❖ Set Positive Financial Goals: Define clean, manageable economic dreams that inspire you to take action. Having a feel of cause can help counteract emotions of pressure and hopelessness.

6. Educate Yourself About Finances

- ❖ Improve Financial Literacy: Invest time in gaining knowledge of approximately private finance through books, podcasts, or on line publications. Understanding economic principles can empower you to make informed selections and decrease anxiety.

- ❖ Seek Professional Help: If monetary pressure feels overwhelming, don't forget consulting a financial guide or counselor. They can provide personalized steering and strategies tailored for your state of affairs.

7. Practice Mindfulness and Stress Management

- ❖ Incorporate Mindfulness Techniques: Engage in mindfulness practices together with meditation, deep breathing physical games, or yoga. These practices can assist lessen strain and improve emotional law.
- ❖ Establish Healthy Routines: Create day by day workouts that include time for self care, bodily activity, and relaxation. Taking care of your intellectual and

physical health can beautify your capability to manage economic strain.

8. Limit Comparisons and Social Media Influence

- ❖ Avoid Social Comparisons: Be mindful of comparing your monetary state of affairs to others, mainly on social media. Remember that everyone's financial journey is specific, and focusing to your progress is greater crucial.
- ❖ Curate Your Online Environment: Follow accounts that promote effective financial conduct and mindfulness as opposed to those who encourage consumerism or competition.

9. Communicate Openly with Loved Ones

- ❖ Share Your Financial Concerns: Talk openly with trusted pals or own family participants about your monetary stress. Sharing your emotions can provide emotional assist and help you experience less remoted.

- ❖ Involve Your Family in Financial Planning: If you share finances with a partner or own family, contain them in budgeting and goal setting discussions. Collaborative planning can alleviate stress and create a feel of shared duty.

10. Celebrate Progress and Small Wins

- ❖ Acknowledge Achievements: Take time to rejoice economic milestones, irrespective of how small. Recognizing your progress can raise motivation and beef up advantageous behaviors.
- ❖ Maintain a Positive Outlook: Focus at the advantageous modifications you're making, and be affected person with your self all through the technique. Remember that breaking loose from

financial pressure is a adventure that takes time.

www.ingramcontent.com/pod-product-compliance
Lightning Source LLC
Chambersburg PA
CBHW070350230526
45471CB00006B/2499